YOUR INVISIBLE POWER

GENEVIEVE BEHREND

SANAGE
PUBLISHING HOUSE

Paperback: 978-939411250-6

Any references to historical events, real people, or real places are used fictitiously. Names, characters, and places are products of the author's imagination.

Printed by:

Sanage Publishing House LLP
Mumbai, India

sanagepublishing@gmail.com

Geneviève Behrend (1881 in Paris – 1960 in United States) was a French-born author and teacher of Mental Science, a New Thought discipline taught by Thomas Troward.

CONTENTS

Foreword

These pages have been written with purpose and hope that their suggestions may furnish you a key to open up the way to the attainment of your desires, and to explain that Fear should be entirely banished from your effort to obtain possession of the things you desire. This presupposes, of course, that your desire for possession is based upon your aspiration for greater liberty. For example, you feel that the possession of more money, lands or friends will make you happier, and your desire for possession of these things arises from a conviction that their possession will bring you liberty and happiness.

In your effort to possess you will discover that the thing you most and ultimately need is to "Be," always (not spasmodically) your best self -that self which understands that the mistakes of those you love are simply misunderstandings. Your feelings that greater possessions, no matter of what kind they may be, will, of themselves bring you contentment or happiness, is a misunderstanding. No person, place or thing can give you happiness. They may give you cause for happiness and a feeling of contentment, but the joy of Living comes from within. Therefore, it is here recommended, rather than otherwise, that you should make the effort to obtain the things which you feel will bring you joy, provided, as previously stated, that your desires are in accord with the joy of Living.

It is also desired, in this volume, to suggest the possibilities in store for all who make persistent effort to understand the Law of Visualization and make practical application of this knowledge on whatever plane he or she may be. The word "effort," as here employed, is not intended to convey the idea of strain. All study and meditation should be without strain or tension.

It has been my endeavor to show that by starting at the beginning of the creative action or the mental picture, certain corresponding results are sure to follow. "While the laws of the Universe cannot be altered, they can be made to work under specific conditions, thereby producing results for individual advancement which cannot be obtained under the spontaneous working of the law provided by Nature."

However far the suggestions I have given you of the possibilities in store for you through visualizing may carry you beyond your past experience, they nowhere break the continuity of the law of cause and effect.

If through the suggestions here given anyone is brought to realize that their mind is a center through and in which "all power there is" is in operation, simply waiting to be given direction in the one and only way through which it can take specific action (and this means reaction in concrete or physical form), then the mission to which this book is dedicated has been fulfilled.

Try to remember that the picture you think, feel and see is reflected into the Universal Mind, and by the natural law of reciprocal action must return to you in either spiritual or physical form. Knowledge of this law of reciprocal action between the individual and the Universal Mind opens to you free access to all you may wish to possess or to be.

It must be steadfastly borne in mind that all this can only be true for the individual who recognizes that they derive their power to make an abiding mental picture from the All-Originating

Universal Spirit of Life (God) and can be used constructively only so long as it is employed and retained in harmony with the Nature of the Spirit which originated it. To insure this there must be no inversion of the thought of the individual regarding their relationship to this Universal Originating Spirit, which is that of a son or daughter, through which the parent mind acts and reacts.

Thus conditioned, whatever you think and feel yourself to be; the Creative Spirit of Life is bound to faithfully reproduce in a corresponding reaction. This is the great reason for picturing yourself and your affairs as you wish them to be as existing facts (though invisible to the physical eye) and live in your picture. An honest endeavor to do this, always recognizing that your own mind is a projection of the Originating Spirit, will prove to you that the best there is, is yours in all your ways.

CHAPTER 1

Order of Visualization

The exercise of the visualizing faculty keeps your mind in order and attracts to you the things you need to make life more enjoyable in an orderly way. If you train yourself in practice of deliberately picturing your desire and carefully examining it, you will soon find your thought and desires come and proceed in more orderly procession than ever before. Having reached a state of ordered mentality you are no longer in a constant state of mental hurry. Hurry is Fear and consequently destructive.

In other words, when your understanding grasps the power to visualize your heart's desire and hold it with your will, it attracts to you all things requisite to the fulfillment of that picture by the harmonious vibrations of the law of attraction. You realize that since Order is Heaven's first law, and visualization places things in their natural element, then it must be a heavenly thing to visualize.

Everyone visualizes, whether they know it or not. Visualizing is the great secret of Success. The conscious use of this great power attracts to you greatly multiplied resources, intensifies your wisdom, and enables you to make use of advantages which you formerly failed to recognize.

We now fly through the air, not because anyone has been able to change the laws of Nature, but because the inventor of the flying machine learned how to apply Nature's laws and, by making orderly use of them, produced the desired result. So far as natural forces are concerned, nothing has changed since the beginning. There were no airplanes in "the Year One," because those of that generation could not conceive the idea as a practical working possibility. "It has not yet been done" was the argument, "and it cannot be done." Yet the laws and materials for practical flying machines existed then as now.

Troward tells us that the great lesson he learned from the airplane and wireless telegraphy is the triumph of principle over precedent, and the working of an idea to its logical conclusion in spite of accum ulated testimony of all past experience.

With such an example before you, can you not realize that still greater secrets may be disclosed? Also "That you hold the key within yourself, with which to unlock the secret chamber that contains your heart's desire? All that is necessary in order that you may use this key and make your life exactly what you wish it to be, is a careful inquiry into the unseen causes which stand back of every external and visible condition. Then bring these unseen causes into harmony with your conception, and you will find that you can make practical working realities of possibilities which at present seem but fantastic dreams."

We all know that the balloon was the forefather of the airplane. In 1766 Henry Cavendish, an English nobleman, proved that hydrogen gas was seven times lighter than atmospheric air. From that discovery the balloon came into existence, and from the ordinary balloon the dirigible, a cigar-shaped airship, was evolved. Study of aeronautics and the laws of aerial locomotion of birds and projectiles led to the belief that mechanism could be evolved by which heavier-than-air machines could be made to travel from place to place and remain in the air by the maintenance of great speed which would overcome by propulsive force the ordinary law of gravitation.

Professor Langley of Washington who developed much of the theory which others afterward improved was subjected to much derision when he sent a model airplane up only to have it bury its nose in the muddy water of the Potomac. But the Wright Brothers, who experimented in the latter part of the Nineteenth Century, realized the possibility of traveling through the air in a machine that had no gas bag. They saw themselves enjoying this mode of transportation with great facility. It is said that one of the brothers would tell the other (when their varied experiments did not turn out as they expected): "It's all right, brother, I can see myself riding in that machine, and it travels easily and steadily." Those Wright Brothers knew what they wanted and kept their pictures constantly before them.

In visualizing, or making, a mental picture, you are not endeavoring to change the laws of Nature. You are fulfilling them. Your object in visualizing is to bring things into regular order both mentally and physically. When you realize that this method of employing the creative power brings your desires, one after another, into practical material accomplishment, your confidence in the mysterious but unfailing law of attraction, which has its central power station in the very heart of your word/picture, becomes supreme. Nothing can shake it. You never feel that it is necessary to take anything from anybody else. You have learned that asking and seeking have receiving and finding as their correlatives. You know that all you have to do is to start the plastic substance of the Universe flowing into the thought-molds your picture- desire provides.

CHAPTER 2

How To Attract To Yourself The Things You Desire

The power within you which enables you to form a thought picture is the starting point of all there is. In its original state it is the undifferentiated formless substance of life. Your thought picture forms the mould (so to speak) into which this formless substance takes shape. Visualizing, or mentally seeing things and conditions as you wish them to be, is the condensing, the specializing power in you that might be illustrated by the lens of a magic lantern. The magic lantern is one of the best symbols of this imaging faculty. It illustrates the working of the Creative Spirit on the plane of the initiative and selection (or in its concentrated specializing form) in a remarkably clear manner.

This picture slide illustrates your own mental picture -invisible in the lantern of your mind until you turn on the light of your will. That is to say, you light up your desire with absolute faith that the Creative Spirit of Life, in you, is doing the work. By the steady flow of light of the will on the Spirit, your desired picture is projected upon the screen of the physical world, an exact reproduction of the pictured slide in your mind.

Visualizing without a will sufficiently steady to inhibit every thought and feeling contrary to your picture would be as useless as a magic lantern without the light. On the other hand, if your will is sufficiently developed to hold your picture in thought and feeling, without any "ifs," simply realizing that your thought is the great attracting power, then your mental picture is as certain to be projected upon the screen of your physical world as any pictured slide put into the best magic lantern ever made.

Try projecting the picture in a magic lantern with a light that is constantly shifting from one side to the other, and you will have the effect of an uncertain will. It is as necessary that you should always stand back of your picture with a strong, steady will, as it is to have a strong steady light back of a picture slide.

The joyous assurance with which you make your picture is the very powerful magnet of Faith, and nothing can obliterate it. You are happier than you ever were, because you have learned to know where your source of supply is, and you rely upon its never-failing response to your given direction.

When all said and done, happiness is the one thing which every human being wants, and the study of visualization enables you to get more out of life than you ever enjoyed before. Increasing possibilities keep opening out, more and more, before you.

A businessman once told me that since practicing visualization and forming the habit of devoting a few minutes each day to thinking about his work as he desired it to be in a large, broad way, his business had more than doubled in six months. His method was to go into a room every morning before breakfast and take a mental inventory of his business as he had left it the evening before, and then enlarge upon it. He said he expanded and expanded in this way until his affairs were in remarkably successful condition. He would see himself in his office doing everything that he wanted done. His occupation required him to meet many strangers every day. In his mental picture he saw himself meeting these people, understanding their needs and supplying them in just the way they wished. This habit, he said, had strengthened and steadied his will in an almost inconceivable manner.

Furthermore, by thus mentally seeing things as he wished them to be, he had acquired the confident feeling that a certain creative power was exercising itself, for him and through him, for the purpose of improving his little world.

When you first begin to visualize seriously, you may feel, as many others do, that someone else may be forming the same picture you are, and that naturally would not suit your purpose. Do not give yourself any unnecessary concern about this. Simply try to realize that your picture is an orderly exercise of the Universal Creative Power specifically applied. Then you may be sure that no one can work in opposition to you. The universal law of harmony prevents this. Endeavor to bear in mind that your mental picture is Universal Mind exercising its inherent powers of initiative and selection specifically.

God, or Universal Mind, made man for the special purpose of differentiating Himself through him. Everything that is, came into existence in this same way, by this self-same law of self-differentiation, and for the same purpose. First the idea, the mental picture or the prototype of the thing, which is the thing itself in its incipiency or plastic form.

The Great Architect of the Universe contemplated Himself as manifesting through His polar opposite, matter, and the idea expanded and projected itself until we have a world-many worlds.

Many people ask, "But why should we have a physical world at all?" The answer is: Because it is the nature of originating substance to solidify, under directivity rather than activity, just as it is the nature of wax to harden when it becomes cold, or plaster of Paris to become firm and solid when exposed to the air. Your picture in this same Divine substance in its fluent state taking shape through the individualized center of Divine operation, your mind; and there is no power to prevent this combination of spiritual substance from becoming physical form. It is the nature of Spirit to complete its work and an idea is not complete until it has made for itself a vehicle.

Nothing can prevent your picture from coming into concrete form except the same power that gave it birth - yourself. Suppose you wish to have a more orderly room. You look about your room and the idea of order suggests boxes, closets, shelves, hooks and so forth. The box, the closet, the hooks, all are concrete ideas of order. Vehicles through which order and harmony suggest themselves.

CHAPTER 3

Relation Between Mental And Physical Form

Some persons feel that it is not quite proper to visualize for things. "It's too material" they say. But material form is necessary for the self-recognition of spirit from the individual standpoint. And this is the means through which the creative process is carried forward. Therefore, far from matter being an illusion and something that ought not to be (as some metaphysical teachers have taught), matter is the necessary channel for the self-differentiation of spirit. However, it is not my desire to lead you into lengthy and tiresome scientific reasoning in order to remove the mystery of visualization and to put it upon a logical foundation. Naturally, each individual will do this in his own way. My only wish is to point out to you the smoothest way I know, which is the road on which Troward guides me. I feel sure you will conclude as I have, that the only mystery in connection with visualizing is the mystery of life taking form, governed by unchangeable and easily understood laws.

We all possess more power and greater possibilities than we realize, and visualizing is one of the greatest of these powers. It brings other possibilities to our observation. When we pause to think for a moment, we realize that for a cosmos to exist at all, it must be the outcome of a cosmic mind, which binds "all individual minds to a certain generic unity of action, thereby producing all things as realities and nothing as illusions." If you will take this thought of Troward's and meditate upon it without prejudice, you will surely realize that concrete material form is an absolute necessity of the creative process, also "that matter is not an illusion but a necessary channel through which life differentiates itself."

If you consider matter in its right order as the polar opposite to Spirit, you will not find any antagonism between them. On the contrary, together they constitute one harmonious whole. And when you realize this, you feel in your practice of visualizing, that you are working from cause to effect, from beginning to finish. In reality your mental picture is the specialized working of the originating spirit.

One could talk for hours on purely scientific lines, showing, as Troward says, "that raw material for the formation of the solar systems is universally distributed throughout all space. Yet investigation shows that while the Heavens are studded with millions of suns, there are spaces that show no signs of cosmic activity. This being true, there must be something which started cosmic activity in certain places, while passing over others in which the raw material was equally available. At first thought one might attribute the development of cosmic energy to the etheric particles themselves. Upon investigation, however, we find this to be mathematically impossible in a medium which is equally distributed throughout space, for all its particles are in equilibrium, therefore no one particle possesses in itself a greater power of originating motion than the other.

Thus, we find that the initial movement, though working in and through the particles of primary substance, is not the particles themselves. It is this something we mean when we speak of Spirit. The same power that brought universal substance into existence will bring your individual thought or mental picture into physical form. There is no difference of kind in the power. The only difference is a difference of scale. The power and the substance themselves are the same. Only in working out your mental picture it has transferred its creative energy from the universal to the scale of the particular and is working in the same unfailing manner from its specific center, your mind.

CHAPTER 4

Operation Of Your Mental Picture

The operation of a large telephone system may be used as a simile. The main or head central subdivides itself into many branch centrals, every branch being in direct connection with its source and each individual branch recognizing the source of its existence, reports all things to its central head. Therefore, when assistance of any nature is required, new supplies, difficult repairs to be done or what not, the branch in need goes at once to its central head. It would not think of referring its difficulties (or its successes) to the main central of a telegraph system (though they belong to the same organization). These different branch centrals know that the only remedy for any difficulty must come from the central out of which they were projected.

If we, as individual branches of the Universal Mind, would refer our difficulties in the same confident manner to the source from which we were projected, and use the remedies that it has provided, we would realize what Jesus meant when he said, "Ask and ye shall receive." Our every equipment would be met. Surely the father must supply the child. The trunk of the tree cannot fail to provide for its branches.

Everything animate or inanimate is called into existence or outstanding-ness by a power which itself does not stand out. The power that creates the mental picture, the originating spirit substance of your pictured desire does not stand out. It projects the substance of itself that is a solidified counterpart of itself, while it remains invisible to the physical eye. Only those will ever appreciate the value of visualizing who are able to realize Paul's meaning when he said "The worlds were formed by the word of God. Things which are seen are not made of things which do appear."

There is nothing unusual or mysterious in the idea of your pictured desire coming into material evidence. It is the working of a universal natural Law.

The world was projected by the self-contemplation of the Universal Mind, and this same action is taking place in its individualized branch which is the Mind of Man. Everything in the whole world has its beginning in mind and comes into existence in exactly the same manner from the hat on your head to the boots on your feet. All are projected thoughts, solidified.

Your personal advance in evolution depends upon your right use of the power of visualizing, and your use of it depends on whether you recognize that you, yourself, are a particular center through and in which the originating spirit is finding ever new expression for potentialities already existing within itself. This is evolution, this continual unfolding of existing though outwardly invisible things.

Your mental picture is the force of attraction that evolves and combines the originating substance into specific shape. Your picture is the combining and evolving powerhouse, so to speak, through which the originating Creative Spirit expressed itself. Its creative action is limitless, without beginning and without end, and always progressive and orderly. "It proceeds stage by stage, each stage being a necessary preparation for the one to follow."

Now let us see if we can get an idea of the different stages by which the things in the world have come to be. Troward says, "If we can get at the working principle which is producing these results, we can very quickly and easily give it personal application. First, we find that the thought of originating life or Spirit about itself is its simple awareness of its own being, and this produced a primary ether, a universal substance out of which everything in the world must grow.

Troward also tells us that "though this awareness of being is a necessary foundation for any further possibilities, it is not much to talk about." It is the same with individualized spirit, which is yourself. Before you would entertain the idea of making a mental picture of your desire as being at all practical, you must have some idea of your being, of your "I am," and just as soon as you are conscious of your "I-am-ness" you begin to wish to enjoy the freedom which this consciousness suggests. You want to do more and be more, and as you fulfill this desire within yourself, localized spirit begins conscious activities in you.

The thing you are most concerned with is the specific action of the creative spirit of life, universal mind specialized. The localized God-germ in you is your personality, your individuality, and since the joy of absolute freedom is the inherent nature of this God-germ, it is natural that it should endeavor to enjoy itself through its specific center. And as you grow in the comprehension that your being, your individuality, is God particularizing Himself, you naturally develop Divine tendencies.

You want to enjoy life and liberty. You want freedom in your affairs as well as in your consciousness, and it is natural that you should. Always with this progressive wish there is a faint thought-picture. As your wish and your recognition grow into an intense desire, this desire becomes a clear mental picture. For example, a young lady studying music wishes she had a piano in order to practice at home. She wants the piano so much that she can mentally see it in one of the rooms. She holds the picture of the piano and indulges in the mental reflection of the pleasure and advantage it will be to have the piano in the corner of the living room. One day she finds it there just as she had pictured it.

As you grow in understanding as to who you are, where you came from, and what the purpose of your being is, how you are to fulfill the purpose for which you are intended, you will more and more afford a center through which the creative spirit of life can enjoy itself. And you will realize that there can be but one creative process filling all space, which is the same in its potentiality whether universal or individual. Furthermore, all that there is, whether on the plane of the visible or invisible, had its origin in the localized action of thought or a mental picture, and this includes yourself, because you are universal spirit localized, and the same creative action is taking place through you.

Now you are no doubt asking yourself why there is so much sickness and misery in the world. If the same power and intelligence which brought the world into existence is in operation in the mind of man, why does it not manifest itself as strength, joy, health and plenty? If one can have one's desires fulfilled by simply making a mental picture of that desire, holding on to it with the will, and doing without anxiety, on the outward plane, whatever seems necessary to bring the desire into fulfillment, then there seems no reason for the existence of sickness and poverty. Surely no one desires either.

The first reason is that few persons will take the trouble to inquire into the working principle of the laws of life. If they did, they would soon convince themselves that there is no necessity for the sickness and poverty that we see about us. They would realize that visualizing is a principle and not a fallacy.

There are a few who have found it worthwhile to study this simple, though absolutely unfailing law that will deliver them from bondage.

However, the race as a whole is not willing to give the time required for this study. It is either too simple, or too difficult. They may make a picture of their desire with some little understanding of visualizing for a day or two, but more frequently it is for an hour or so.

But if you will insist upon mentally seeing yourself surrounded by things and conditions as you wish them to be, you will understand that the creative energy sends its plastic substance in the direction indicated by the tendency of your thoughts. Herein lies the advantage of holding your thought in the form of a mental picture.

The more enthusiasm and faith you are able to put into your picture, the more quickly it will come into visible form, and your enthusiasm is increased by keeping your desire secret. The moment you speak it to any living soul, that moment your power is weakened. Your power, your magnet of attraction is not so strong, and consequently cannot reach so far. The more perfectly a secret between your mind and outer self is guarded, the more vitality you give your power of attraction. One tells one's troubles to weaken them, to get them off one's mind, and when a thought is given out, its power is dissipated. Talk it over with yourself, and even write it down and at once destroy the paper.

However, this does not mean that you should strenuously endeavor to compel the power to work out your picture on the special lines that you think it should. That method would soon exhaust you and hinder the fulfillment of your purpose. A wealthy relative need not necessarily die, or someone lose a fortune on the street to materialize the $10,000 that you are mentally picturing.

One of the doormen in the building in which I live heard much of the mental picturing of desires from visitors passing out of my rooms. The average desire was for $500. He considered that five dollars was more in his line and began to visualize it, without the slightest idea of where or how he was to get it. My parrot flew out of the window, and I telephoned to the men in the courtyard to get it for me. One caught it and it bit him on the finger. The doorman, who had gloves on, and did not fear a similar hurt, took hold of it and brought it up to me. I gave him five one-dollar bills for the service.

This sudden reward surprised him. He enthusiastically told me that he had been visualizing for just $5, merely from hearing that others visualized. He was delighted at the unexpected realization of his mental picture.

All you have to do is to make such a mental picture of your heart's desire, hold it cheerfully in place with your will, always conscious that the same Infinite Power which brought the universe into existence brought you into form for the purpose of enjoying itself in and through you. And since it is all life, love, light, power, peace, beauty and joy, and is the only creative power there is, the form it takes in and through you depends upon the direction given it by your thought indicator. In you it is undifferentiated, waiting to take any direction given it as it passes through the instrument that it has made for the purpose of self-distribution.

It is this power which enables you to transfer your thoughts from one form to another. The power to change your mind is the individualized universal power taking the initiative, giving direction to the fluent substance contained in every thought. It is the simplest thing in the world to give this highly sensitive plastic substance any form you will through visualizing.

Anyone can do it with a small expenditure of effort.

Once you really believe that your mind is a center through which the plastic substance of all there is in your world, takes involuntary form, the only reason why your picture does not always materialize is because you have introduced something antagonistic to the fundamental principle. Very often this destructive element is caused by the frequency with which you change your pictures. After many such changes you decide that your original desire is what you want after all. Upon this conclusion you begin to wonder why, "being your first picture," it hasn't materialized. The plastic substance with which you are mentally dealing is more sensitive than the most sensitive photographer's film. If, in taking a picture, you suddenly remembered you had already taken a picture on that same plate, you would not expect a perfect result of either picture.

On the other hand, you may have taken two pictures on the same plate unconsciously. When the plate has been developed, and the picture comes into physical view, you do not condemn the principle of photography, nor are you puzzled to understand why your picture has turned out so unsatisfactorily. You do not feel that it is impossible for you to obtain a good, clear picture of the subject in question. You know that you can do so, by simply starting at the beginning, putting in a new plate, and determining to be more careful while taking your picture next time. These lines followed out you are sure of a satisfactory result. If you will proceed in the same manner with your mental picture, doing your part in a correspondingly confident frame of mind, the result will be just as perfect.

The laws of visualizing are as infallible as the laws governing photography. In fact, photography is the outcome of visualizing. Again, your results in visualizing and your desires may be imperfect or delayed through the misuse of this power, owing to the thought that the fulfillment of your desire is contingent upon certain persons or conditions. The originating principle is not in any way dependent upon any person, place or thing. It has no past and knows no future.

The law is that the originating creative principle of life is "the universal here and everlasting now." It creates its own vehicles through which to operate. Therefore, past experience has no bearing upon your present picture. So do not try to obtain your desire through a channel that may not be natural for it, even though it may seem reasonable to you. Your feeling should be that the thing, or the consciousness which you so much desire, is normal and natural, a part of yourself, a form for your evolution. If you can do this, there is no power to prevent your enjoying the fulfillment of the picture you have in hand, or any other.

CHAPTER 5

Expressions from Beginners

Hundreds of persons have realized that "visualizing is an Aladdin's lamp to him with a mighty will." General Foch says that his feelings were so outraged during the Franco Prussian war in 1870 that he visualized himself leading a French army against the Germans to victory. He said he made his picture, smoked his pipe and waited. This is one result of visualizing we are all familiar with.

A famous actress wrote a long article in one of the leading Sunday papers last winter's describing how she rid herself of excessive body fat and weight by seeing her figure constantly as she wished to be.

A very interesting letter came to me from a doctor's wife while I was lecturing in New York. She began with the hope that I would never discontinue my lectures on visualization making humanity realize the wonderful fact that they possess the method of liberation within themselves. Relating her own experience, she said that she had been born on the East Side of New York in the poorest quarter. From earliest girlhood she had cherished a dream of marrying a physician someday. This dream gradually formed a stationary mental picture. The first position she obtained was in the capacity of a nursemaid in a physician's family.

Leaving this place, she entered the family of another doctor. The wife of her employer died, and in time the doctor married her, the result of her long- pictured yearning. After that both she and her husband conceived the idea of owning a fruit farm in the South. They formed a mental picture of the idea and put their faith in its eventual fulfillment. The letter she sent me came from their fruit farm in the South. It was while at the farm that the doctor's wife wrote me. Her second mental picture had seen the light of materialization.

Many letters of a similar nature come to me every day. The following is a case that was printed in the New York Herald last May:

Atlantic City, May 5

She was an old woman, and when she was arraigned before Judge Clarence Goldenberg in the police court today, she was so weak and tired she could hardly stand. The judge asked the court attendant what she was charged with.

"Stealing a bottle of milk, Your Honor," repeated the officer. "She took it from the doorstep of a downtown cottage before daybreak this morning."

"Why did you do that?" Judge Goldenberg asked her.

"I was hungry," the old woman said. "I didn't have a cent in the world and no way to get anything to eat except to steal it. I didn't think anybody would mind if I took a bottle of milk."

"What's your name?" asked the judge.

"Weinberg," said the old woman, "Elizabeth Weinberg."

Judge Goldenberg asked her a few questions about herself. Then he said: "Well, you're not very wealthy now, but you're no longer poor. I've been searching for you for months. I've got $500 belonging to you from the estate of a relative. I am the executor of the estate."

Judge Goldenberg paid the woman's fine out of his own pocket, and then escorted her into his office, where he turned her legacy over to her and sent a policeman out to find her a lodging place.

I learned later that this little woman had been desiring and mentally picturing $500, while all the time ignorant of how it could possibly come to her. But she kept her vision and strengthened it with her faith.

In a recent issue of Good Housekeeping there was an article by Addington Bruce entitled "Stiffening Your Mental Backbone." It is very instructive and would benefit anyone to read it. He says, in part: "Form the habit of devoting a few moments every day to thinking about your work in a large, broad imaginative way, as a vital necessity to yourself and a useful service to society."

Huntington, the great railway magnate, before he started building his road from coast to coast, said that he took hundreds of trips all along the line before there was a rail laid. It is said that he would sit for hours with a map of the United States before him and mentally travel from coast to coast just as we do now over his fulfilled mental picture. It would be possible to call your attention to hundreds of similar cases.

The best method of picturing to yourself that which you may desire is both simple and enjoyable, if you once understand the principle back of it well enough to believe it. First and above everything else, be sure of what it is you really want. Then specialize your desire along these lines.

CHAPTER 6

Suggestions for Making Your Mental Picture

Perhaps you want to feel that you've lived to some purpose. You want to be content and happy, and you feel that with good health and with successful business you could enjoy this state of mind. After you have decided once and for all that this is what you want, you proceed to picture yourself healthy, and your business just as great a success as you can naturally conceive it growing into.

The best time for making your definite picture is just before breakfast and before retiring at night. As it is necessary to give yourself plenty of time, it may be necessary to rise earlier than is your usual habit. Go into a room where you will not be disturbed, meditate for a few moments upon the practical working of the law of visualizing, and ask yourself, "How did the things about me first come into existence. How may I find it helpful to get more quickly in touch with the invisible supply?"

Someone felt that comfort would be better expressed and experienced by sitting on a chair than on the floor. The very beginning of the meditation, the chair, was the desire to be at ease. With this came the picture of some sort of a chair. The same principle applies to the hat and the clothes that you wear. Go carefully into this thought of the principle back of the thing.

Establish it as a personal experience; make it a fact to your consciousness.

If you are thorough in this, you will find yourself in the deep consciousness beneath the surface of your own thought-power. Then open a window, take about ten deep breaths, and during the time draw a large imaginary circle of light around you. As you inhale (keeping yourself in the center of this circle of light) see great rays of light coming from the circle and entering your body at all points, centralizing itself at your solar plexus.

Hold the breath a few moments at this central light of your body (the solar plexus) then slowly exhale. As you do this mentally, see imaginary rays, or sprays, of light going up through the body and down and out through the feet. Mentally spray your entire body with this imaginary light. When you have finished the breathing exercise, sit in a comfortable upright chair and mentally know there is but one life, one substance, and this life substance of the universe is finding pleasure in self-recognition in you. Repeat some affirmation of this kind, until you feel the truth and reality of the words that you are affirming. Then begin your picture.

Whether your desire is for a state of consciousness or a possession, large or small, begin at the beginning. If you want a house, begin by seeing yourself in the kind of house you desire. Go all through it, taking careful note of the rooms, where the windows are situated, and such other details as help you to feel the reality of your concept.

You might change some of the furniture and look into some of the mirrors just to see how healthy, wealthy and happy you look. Go over your picture again and again until you feel the reality of it, then write it all down just as you have seen it, with the feeling that, "The best there is, is mine. There is no limit to me, because my mind is a center of divine operation" and your picture is as certain to come true, in your physical world, as the sun is to shine.

CHAPTER 7

Things to Remember

In Using Your Thought Power for the Production of New Conditions,

1. Be sure to know what conditions you wish to produce. Then weigh carefully to what further results the accomplishment of your desire will lead.

2. By letting your thought dwell upon a mental picture, you are concentrating the creative spirit to this center, where all its forces are equally balanced.

3. Visualizing brings your objective mind into a state of equilibrium which enables you to consciously direct the flow of spirit to a definitely recognized purpose and to carefully guide your thought from including a flow in the opposite direction.

4. You must always bear in mind that you are dealing with a wonderful potential energy -which is not yet differentiated into any particular mould, and that by the action of your

mind you can differentiate it into any specific mould that you will. Your picture assists you to keep your mind fixed on the fact that the inflow of this creative energy is taking place. Also, by your mental picture you are determining the direction you wish the sensitive creative power to take, and by doing this the externalization of your picture is a certainty.

5. Remember when you are visualizing properly that there is no strenuous effort on your thoughts to hold your thought-forms in place. Strenuous effort defeats your purpose and suggests the consciousness of an adverse force to be fought against, and this creates conditions adverse to your picture.

6. By holding your picture in a cheerful frame of mind, you shut out all thoughts that would disperse the spiritual nucleus of your picture. Because the law is creative in its action, your pictured desire is certain of accomplishment.

7. The seventh and great thing to remember in visualizing is that you are making a mental picture for the purpose of determining the quality you are giving to the previously undifferentiated substance and energy rather than to arrange the specific circumstances for its manifestation. That is the work of creative power itself. It will build its own forms of expression quite naturally, if you will allow it, and save you a great deal of needless anxiety. What you really want is expansion in a certain direction, whether of health, wealth, or what not, and so long as you get it (as you surely will, if you confidently hold to your picture) what does it matter whether it reaches you by some channel which you thought you could count upon, or through some other of whose existence you had no idea. You are concentrating energy of a particular kind for a particular purpose. Bear this in mind and let specific details take care of themselves, and never mention your intention to anyone.

Remember always, that Nature from her clearly visible surface to her most arcane depths is one vast storehouse of light and good entirely devoted to your individual use. Your conscious Oneness with the great Whole is the secret of success and when once you have fathomed this you can enjoy your possession of the whole or a part of it at will, because by your recognition you have made it, and can increasingly make it yours.

Never forget that every physical thing, whether for you or against you, was a sustained thought before it was a thing.

Thought as thought is neither good nor bad, it is creative action and always takes physical form.

Therefore, the thoughts you dwell upon become the things you possess or do not possess.

CHAPTER 8

Why I Took Up The Study Of Mental Science

I have frequently been questioned about my reasons for taking up the study of Mental Science, and as to the results of my search, not only in knowledge of principles, but also in the application of that knowledge to the development of my own life and experience.

Such inquiries are justifiable, because one who essays the role of a messenger and teacher of psychological truths can only be effective and convincing as he or she has tested them in the laboratory of mental experience. This is particularly true in my case, as the only personal pupil of Thomas Troward, the greatest Master of Mental Science of the present day, whose teaching is based upon the relation borne by the Individual Mind toward the Universal Creative Mind which is the Giver of Life, and the manner in which that relation may be invoked to secure expansion and fuller expression in the individual life.

The initial impulse toward the study of Mental Science was an overwhelming sense of loneliness. In every life there must come some such experiences of spiritual isolations as, at that period, pervaded my life.

Notwithstanding the fact that each day found me in the midst of friends, surrounded by mirth and gayety, there was a persistent feeling that I was alone in the world. I had been a widow for about three years, wandering from country to country, seeking for peace of mind.

The circumstances and surroundings of my life were such that my friends looked upon me as an unusually fortunate young woman. Although they recognized that I had sustained a great loss when my husband died, they knew that he had left me well provided for, free to go anywhere at pleasure, and having many friends. Yet, if my friends could have penetrated my inmost emotions, they would have found a deep sense of emptiness and isolation.

This feeling inspired a spirit of unrest that drove me on and on in fruitless search upon the outside for that which I later learned could only be obtained from within.

I studied Christian Science, but it gave me no solace, though fully realizing the great work the Scientists were doing, and even having the pleasure and privilege of meeting Mrs. Eddy personally. But it was impossible for me to accept the fundamental teachings of Christian Science and make practical application of it.

When about to abandon the search for contentment and resign myself to resume a life of apparent amusement, a friend invited me to visit the great Seer and Teacher, Abdul Baha. After my interview with this most wonderful of men, my search for contentment began to take a change. He had told me that I would travel the world over seeking the truth, and when I had found it would speak it out. The fulfillment of the statement of this Great Seer then seemed to be impossible. But it carried a measure of encouragement, and at least indicated that my former seeking had been in the wrong direction. I began in a feeble and groping way to find contentment within myself, for had he not intimated that I should find the truth. That was the big thing, and about the only thing I remember of our interview.

A few days later, upon visiting the office of a New Thought practitioner, my attention was attracted to a book on his table entitled "The Edinburgh Lectures on Mental Science," by Thomas Troward. It interested me to see that Troward was a retired Divisional judge from the Punjab, India. I purchased the book, thinking I would read it through that evening. Many have endeavored to do the same thing, only to find, as I did, that the book must be studied in order to be understood, and hundreds have decided, just as I did, to give it their undivided attention.

After finding this treasure book I went to the country for a few days, and while there studied the volume as thoroughly as I could. It seemed extremely difficult, and I decided to purchase another book of Troward's, in the hope that its study might not require so much of an effort. Upon inquiry I was told that a subsequent volume, "The Dore Lectures," was much the simpler and better of the two books. When I procured it, I found that it must also be studied. It took me weeks and months to get even a vague conception of the meaning of the first chapter of Dore, which is entitled "Entering into the Spirit of It." I mean by this that it took me months to enter into the spirit of what I was reading.

But in the meantime, a paragraph from page 26 arrested my attention, as seeming the greatest thing I had ever read. I memorized it and endeavored with all my soul to enter into the spirit of Troward's words. The paragraph reads: "My mind is a center of Divine operation. The Divine operation is always for expansion and fuller expression, and this means the production of something beyond what has gone before, something entirely new, not included in the past experience, though proceeding out of it by an orderly sequence of growth. Therefore, since the Divine cannot change its inherent nature, it must operate in the same manner with me; consequently, in my own special world, of which I am the center, it will move forward to produce new conditions, always in advance of any that have gone before."

It took an effort on my part to memorize this paragraph, but in the endeavor toward this end the words seemed to carry with them a certain stimulus. Each repetition of the paragraph made it easier for me to enter into the spirit of it. The words expressed exactly what I had been seeking for. My one desire was for peace of mind. I found it comforting to believe that the Divine operation in me could expand to fuller expression and produce more and more contentment in fact, a peace of mind and a degree of contentment greater than I had ever known. The paragraph further inspired me with deep interest to feel that the life-spark in me could bring into my life something entirely new. I did not wish to obliterate my past experience, but that was exactly what Troward said it would not do. The Divine operation would not exclude my past experience but proceeding out of them would bring some new thing that would transcend anything that I had ever experienced before.

Meditation on these statements brought with it a certain joyous feeling. What a wonderful thing it would be if I could accept and sincerely believe, beyond all doubt, that this one statement of Troward's was true. Surely the Divine could not change its inherent nature, and since Divine life is operating in me, I must be Divinely inhabited, and the Divine in me must operate just as it operates upon the Universal plane. This meant that my whole world of circumstances, friends and conditions would ultimately become a world of contentment and enjoyment of which "I am the center." This would all happen just as soon as I was able to control my mind and thereby provide concrete center around which the Divine energies could play.

Surely it was worth trying for. If Troward had found this truth, why not I? The idea held me to my task. Later I determined to study with the man who had realized and given to the world so great a statement. It had lifted me from my state of despondency. The immediate difficulty was the need for

---

CHAPTER 9

How I Attracted To Myself Twenty Thousand Dollars

In the laboratory of experience in which my newly revealed relation to Divine operation was to be tested, the first problem was a financial one. My income was a stipulated one, quite enough for my everyday needs. But it did not seem sufficient to enable me to go comfortably to England where Troward lived and remain for an indefinite period to study with so great a teacher as he must be. So before inquiring whether Troward took pupils or whether I would be eligible in case he did, I began to use the paragraph I had memorized. Daily, in fact, almost hourly, the words were in my mind: "My mind is a center of Divine operation, and Divine operation means expansion into something better than has gone before."

From the Edinburgh Lectures I had read something about the Law of Attraction, and from the Chapter of "Causes and Conditions" I had gleaned a vague idea of visualizing. So, every night, before going to sleep, I made a mental picture of the desired $20,000.

Twenty $1,000 bills were counted over each night in my bedroom, and then, with the idea of more emphatically impressing my mind with the fact that these twenty thousand dollars was for the purpose of going to England and studying with Troward, I wrote out my picture, saw myself buying my steamer ticket, walking up and down the ship's deck from New York to London, and, finally, saw myself accepted as Troward's pupil.

This process was repeated every morning and every evening, always impressing more and more fully upon my mind Troward's memorized statement: "My mind is a center of Divine operations." I endeavored to keep this statement in the back part of my consciousness all the time with no thought in mind as how the money might be obtained. Probably the reason why there was no thought of the avenues through which the money might reach me was because I could not possibly imagine where the $20,000 would come from. So, I simply held my thought steady and let the power of attraction find its own ways and means.

One day while walking on the street, taking deep breathing exercises, the thought came: "My mind is surely a center of Divine operation. If God fills all space, then God must be in my mind also; if I want this money to study with Troward that I may know the truth of Life, then both the money and the truth must be mine, though I am unable to feel or see the physical manifestations of either; still," I declared, "it must be mine."

While these reflections were going on in my mind, there seemed to come up from within me the thought: "I am all the substance there is." Then, from another channel in my brain the answer seemed to come, "Of course, that's it; everything must have its beginning in mind. The "I" the Idea, must be the only one and primary substance there is, and this means money as well as everything else." My mind accepted this idea, and immediately all the tension of mind and body was relaxed.

There was a feeling of absolute certainty of being in touch with all the power Life has to give. All thought of money, teacher, or even my own personality, vanished in the great wave of joy which swept over my entire being. I walked on and on with this feeling of joy steadily increasing and expanding until everything about me seemed aglow with resplendent light. Every person I passed was illuminated as I was. All consciousness of personality had disappeared, and in its place, there came that great and almost overwhelming sense of joy and contentment.

That night when I made my picture of the twenty thousand dollars it was with an entirely changed aspect. On previous occasions, when making my mental picture, I had felt that I was waking up something within myself. This time there was no sensation of effort. I simply counted over the twenty thousand dollars. Then, in a most unexpected manner, from a source of which I had no consciousness at the time, there seemed to open a possible avenue through which the money might reach me.

At first it took great effort not to be excited. It all seemed so wonderful, so glorious to be in touch with supply. But had not Troward cautioned his readers to keep all excitement out of their minds in the first flush of realization of union with Infinite supply, and to treat this fact as a perfectly natural result that had been reached through our demand? This was even more difficult for me than it was to hold the thought that "all the substance there is, I am, I (idea) am the beginning of all form, visible or invisible."

Just as soon as there appeared a circumstance which indicated the direction through which the twenty thousand dollars might come, I not only made a supreme effort to regard the indicated direction calmly as the first sprout of the seed I had sown in the absolute but left no stone unturned to follow up that direction by fulfilling my part. By so doing one circumstance seemed naturally to lead to another, until, step-by-step, my desired twenty thousand dollars was secured. To keep my mind poised and free from excitement was my greatest effort.

This first concrete fruition of my study of Mental Science as expounded by Troward's book had come by a careful following of the methods he had outlined. In this connection, therefore, I can offer to the reader no better gift than to quote Troward's book, "The Edinburgh Lectures," from which may be derived a complete idea of the line of action I was endeavoring to follow. In the chapter on Causes and Conditions he says: "To get good results we must properly understand our relation to the great impersonal power we are using. It is intelligent, and we are intelligent, and the two intelligences must co-operate.

We must not fly in the face of the Law expecting it to do for us what it can only do through us; and we must therefore use our intelligence with the knowledge that it is acting as the instrument of a greater intelligence; and because we have this knowledge we may and should cease from all anxiety as to the final result.

In actual practice we must first form the ideal conception of our object with the definite intention of impressing it upon the universal mind -it is this thought that takes such thought out of the region of mere casual fancies -and then affirm that our knowledge of the Law is sufficient reason for a calm expectation of a corresponding result, and that therefore all necessary conditions will come to us in due order. We can then turn to the affairs of our daily life with the calm assurance that the initial conditions are either there already or will soon come into view. If we do not at once see them, let us rest content with the knowledge that the spiritual prototype is already in existence and wait till some circumstance pointing in the desired direction begins to show itself.

It may be a very small circumstance, but it is the direction and not the magnitude that is to be taken into consideration. As soon as we see it, we should regard it as the first sprouting of the seed sown in the Absolute, and do calmly, and without excitement, whatever the circumstances seem to require, and then later on we shall see that this doing will in turn lead to a further circumstance in the same direction, until we find ourselves conducted, step by step, to the accomplishment of our object.

In this way the understanding of the great principle of the Law of Supply will, by repeated experiences, deliver us more and more completely out of the region of anxious thought and toilsome labor and bring us into a new world where the useful employment of all our powers, whether mental or physical, will only be an unfolding of our individuality upon the lines of its own nature, and therefore a perpetual source of health and happiness; a sufficient inducement, surely, to the careful study of the laws governing the relation between the individual and the Universal Mind."

To my mind, then as now, this quotation outlines the core and center of the method and manner of approach necessary for coming in touch with Infinite supply. At least it, together with the previously quoted statement, "My mind is a center of Divine operation," etc., constituted the only apparent means of attracting to myself the twenty thousand dollars. My constant endeavor to get into the spirit of these statements, and to attract to myself this needed sum, was about six weeks, at the end of which time I had in my bank the required twenty thousand dollars. This could be made into a long story, giving all the details, but the facts, as already narrated, will give you a definite idea of the magnetic condition of my mind while the twenty thousand dollars was finding its way to me.

CHAPTER 10

How I Became The Only Personal Pupil Of The Greatest Mental Scientist Of The Present Day

As soon as the idea of studying with Troward came to me, I asked a friend to write to him for me, feeling that perhaps my friend could put my desire in better or more persuasive terms than I could employ. To all the letters written by this friend I received not one reply. This was so discouraging that I would have completely abandoned the idea of becoming Troward's pupil except for the experience I had that day on the street when my whole world was illuminated, and I remembered the promise "All things whatsoever thou wilt, believe thou hast received, and thou shalt receive."

With this experience in my mind, my passage to England was arranged, notwithstanding the fact that apparently my letters were ignored. We wrote again, however, and finally received a reply, very courteous though very positive. Troward did not take pupils; he had no time to devote to a pupil. Notwithstanding this definite decision, I declined to be discouraged because of the memory of my experience upon the day when the light and the thought came to me, "I am all the Substance there is." I seemed to be able to live that experience over at will, and with it there always came a flood of courage and renewed energy. We journeyed on to London, and from there telegraphed Troward, asking for an interview. The telegram was promptly answered by Troward setting a date when he could see us.

At this time Troward was living in Ruan Manor, a little-out-of-the-way place in the southern part of England, about twenty miles from a railway station. We could not find it on the map, and with great difficulty Cook's Touring Agency in London, located the place for us. There was very little speculation in my mind as to what Troward would say to me in this interview. There always remained the feeling that the truth was mine; also, that it would grow and expand in my consciousness until peace and contentment were outward as well as inward manifestations of my individual life.

We arrived at Troward's house in a terrific rainstorm, and were cordially received by Troward himself, whom I found, much to my surprise, to be more the type of a Frenchman than an Englishman (I afterward learned that he was a descendant of the Huguenot race), a man of medium stature, with rather a large head, big nose, and eyes that fairly danced with merriment. After we had been introduced to the other members of the family and given a hot cup of tea, we were invited into the living room where Troward talked very freely of everything except my proposed studies. It seemed quite impossible to bring him to that subject.

Just before we were leaving, however, I asked quite boldly: "Will you not reconsider your decision to take a personal pupil? I wish so much to study with you," to which he replied with a very indifferent manner that he did not feel he could give the time it would require for personal instruction, but that he would be glad to give me the names of two or three books which he felt would not only be interesting but instructive to me. He said he felt much flattered and pleased that I had come all the way from America to study with him, and as we walked out through the lane from his house to our automobile his manner became less indifferent, a feeling of sympathy seemed to touch his heart, and he turned to me with the remark: "You might write to me, if so inclined, after you get to Paris, and perhaps, if I have time in the autumn, we could arrange something, though it does not seem possible now."

I lost no time in following up his very kind invitation to write. My letters were all promptly and courteously answered, but there was never a word of encouragement as to my proposed studies. Finally, about two months later, there came a letter with the question in it: "What do you suppose is the meaning of this verse in the 21st Chapter of Revelation?"

> *"16. And the city lieth foursquare and the length is as large as the breadth; and he measured the city with the reed, twelve thousand furlongs. The length and the breadth and the height of it are equal."*

Instinctively I knew that my chance to study with Troward hung upon my giving the correct answer to that question. The definition of the verse seemed utterly beyond my reach. Naturally, answers came to my mind, but I knew intuitively that none was correct. I began bombarding my scholarly friends and acquaintances with the same question. Lawyers, doctors, priests, nuns and clergymen, all over the world, received letters from me with this question in them. Later answers began to return to me, but intuition told me that none was correct. All the while I was endeavoring to find the answer for myself, but none seemed to come. I memorized the verse in order that I might meditate upon it.

I began a search of Paris for the books Troward had recommended to me, and after two- or three-days' search, we crossed the River Seine to the Ile de Cite to go into some of the old bookstores there.

They were out of print, and these were the best places to find them in. Finally, we came upon a little shop that had the books there. These were the last copies the man had, consequently the price was high. While remonstrating with the clerk, my eye rested upon the work of an astrologer, which I laughingly picked up and asked: "Do you think Prof. would read my horoscope?" The clerk looked aghast at the suggestion, and responded, "Why, no, Madame, this is one of France's greatest astrologers. He does not read horoscopes."

In spite of this answer, there was a persistent impulse within me to go to the man. The friend who had accompanied me in my search for the books remonstrated with me and tried in every way to dissuade me from going to the famous astrologer, but I insisted, and she went with me. When we came to his office, I found it somewhat embarrassing to ask him to read my horoscope. Nevertheless, there was nothing to do but put the question. Reluctantly, the Professor invited us into his paper-strewn study, and reluctantly, and also impatiently, asked us to be seated. Very courteously and coldly he told me that he did not read horoscopes. His whole manner said, more clearly than words could, that he wished we would take our departure.

My friend stood up. I was at a great loss what to do next, because I felt that I was not quite ready to go. Intuition seemed to tell me there was something for me to gain there. Just what it was I was unable to define, so I paused a moment, much to my friend's displeasure, when one of the Professor's enormous Persian cats jumped into my lap. "Get down, Jack!" the Professor shouted. "What does it mean?" he seemed to ask himself. Then with a greater interest than he had hitherto shown in me, the Professor said with a smile: "Have never known that cat to go to a stranger before, Madame; my at pleads for you." I, also, now feel an interest in your horoscope, and if you will give me the data it will give me pleasure to write it out for you." There was a great feeling of happiness in me when he made this statement. He concluded by saying: "I do not feel that you really care for your horoscope." The truth of this statement shocked me, because I did not care about a horoscope, and could not give any reason why I was letting him do it. "However," he said, "May I call for your data next Sunday afternoon?"

On Sunday afternoon at the appointed time, the Professor arrived, and I was handing him the slip of paper with all the data of my birth, etc., when the idea came to me to ask the Professor for the answer to the question about the 16th verse of the 21st Chapter of Revelation. The thought was instantly carried into effect, and I found myself asking this man what he thought this verse meant. Without pausing to think it over he immediately replied, "it means: The city signifies the truth, and the truth is non-invertible; every side from which you approach it is exactly the same." Intuitively and undoubtingly, I recognized this answer as the true one, and my joy knew no bounds, because I felt sure that with this correct answer in my possession, Troward would accept me as his pupil in the fall.

As the great astrologer was leaving, I explained to him all about my desire to study with Troward, how I had come from New York City for that express purpose, seemingly to no avail, until the answer to this test question had been given to me by him. He was greatly interested and asked many questions about Troward, and when asked if he would please send me his bill, he smilingly replied, "Let me know if the great Troward accepts you as his pupil," and bade me good afternoon. I hastened to my room to send a telegram to Troward giving my answer to the question about the 16th verse of the 21st Chapter of Revelation.

There was an immediate response from Troward that said: "Your answer is correct. Am beginning a course of lectures on The Great Pyramid in London. If you wish to attend them, will be pleased to have you, and afterward, if you still wish to study with me, I think it can be arranged." On receipt of this reply preparations were at once made to leave Paris for London.

I attended all the lectures, receiving much instruction from them, after which arrangements were made for my studying with Troward. Two days before leaving for Cornwall I received the following letter from Troward clearly indicating the line of study he gave me:

31 Stanwick Road,
W. Kensington, England,
November 8, 1912.

Dear Mrs. Behrend,

I think I had better write you a few lines with regard to your proposed studies with me, as I should be sorry for you to be under any misapprehension and so to suffer any disappointment.

I have studied the subject now for several years, and have a general acquaintance with the leading features of most of the systems which, unfortunately, occupy attention in many circles at the present time, such as Theosophy, The Tarot, The Kabala, and the like, and I have no hesitation in saying that, to the best of my judgment, all sorts and descriptions of so- called occult study are in direct opposition to the real life-giving Truth, and, therefore, you must not expect any teaching on such lines as these.

We hear a great deal these days about Initiation; but, believe me, the more you try to become a so-called "Initiate" the further you will put yourself from living life. I speak after many years of careful study and consideration when I say that the Bible and its Revelation of Christ is the one thing really worth studying, and that is a subject large enough in all conscience, embracing, as it does, our outward life and of everyday concerns, and also the inner springs of our life and all that we can in general terms conceive of the life in the unseen after putting off the body at death.

You have expressed a very great degree of confidence in my teaching, and if your confidence is such that you wish, as you say, to put yourself entirely under my guidance, I can only accept it as a very serious responsibility, and should have to ask you to exhibit that confidence by refusing to look into such so-called "Mysteries" as I would forbid you to look into.

I am speaking from experience; but the result will be that much of my teaching will appear to be very simple, perhaps to some extent dogmatic, and you will say you have heard much of it before.

Faith in God, Prayer and Worship, approach to the Father through Christ all this is in a certain sense familiar to you; and all I can hope to do is perhaps to throw a little more-light on these subjects, that they may become to you, not merely traditional words, but present living facts.

I have been thus explicit as I do not want you to have any disappointment, and also, I should say that our so-called course of study will be only friendly conversations at such times as we can fit them in, either you coming to our house, or I to yours, as may be most convenient at the time.

Also, I will lend you some books that will be helpful, but they are very few, and in no sense occult.

Now, if all this falls in with your ideas, we shall, I am sure, be very glad to see you at Ruan Manor, and you will find that the residents there, though few, are very friendly and the neighborhood very pretty.

But, on the other hand, if you feel that you want some other source of learning, do not mind saying so, only you will never find any substitute for Christ.

I trust you will not mind my writing you like this, but I do not want you to come all the way down to Cornwall, and then be disappointed.

With kindest regards,
Yours sincerely,

(Signed) T. TROWARD.

This copy of Troward's letter, to my mind, is the greatest thing I can give you.

CHAPTER 11

How To Bring The Power In Your Word Into Action

In your every word there is the power germ that expands and projects itself in the direction your word indicates, and ultimately develops into physical expression. For example, you wish to establish joy in your consciousness. Just repeat the word "joy" secretly, persistently and emphatically. The joy germ begins to expand and project itself until your whole being is filled with joy. This is not a mere fancy, but a truth. Once you experience this power, you will "daily prove that these facts have not been fabricated to fit a theory, but the theory has been built up by careful observation of facts." Everyone knows that joy comes from within. Another may give you cause for joy, but no one can be joyous for you. Joy is a state of consciousness, and consciousness is purely Troward says, "Mental."

Mental faculties always work under something which stimulates them, and this stimulus may come either from without, through the external senses, or from within by the consciousness of something not perceptible on the physical plane. The recognition of this interior source of stimulus enables you to bring into your consciousness any state you "desire." Once a thing seems normal to you, it is as surely yours, through the law of growth and attraction, as it is yours to know addition after you have the conscious use of figures.

This method of repeating the word makes the word in all of its limitless meaning yours, because words are the embodiment of thoughts, and thought is creative, neither good nor bad, simply creative. This is the reason why Faith builds up and Fear destroys. "Only believe, and all things are possible unto you." It is Faith that gives you dominion over every adverse circumstance or condition. It is your word of faith that sets you free, not faith in any specific thing or act, but simple Faith in your best self in all ways. It is because of this ever-present creative power within the heart of the word that makes your health, your peace of mind and your financial condition a reproduction of your most habitual thought. Try to believe and understand this, and you will find yourself Master of every adverse circumstance or condition, a Prince of Power.

CHAPTER 12

How To Increase Your Faith

But you ask How can I speak the word of Faith when I have little or no faith? Every living thing has faith in something or somebody. It is the quality of the creative energy in the positive Faith thought which gives it vitality, not the form it takes. Even intense fear is alive with faith. You fear smallpox because you believe it possible for you to contract it. You fear poverty and loneliness because you believe them possible for you.

It is your habitual tendency of thought that reappears in your mind, your body and your affairs, not the occasional thought upon some specific line or desire. It is the Faith which understands that every creation had its birth in the womb of thought words that gives you dominion over all things, your lesser self-included, and this feeling of faith is increased and intensified through observing what it does.

This observation is the observation of your state of consciousness when you did, not when you hoped you might, but feared it was too good to be true. How did you feel that time when you simply had to bring yourself into a better frame of mind and did, or you had to have a certain thing and got it? Live these experiences over again and again (mentally) until you really feel in touch with the self that knows and does, and the best there is, is yours.

CHAPTER 13

The Reward Of Increased Faith

Because you have expanded your faith into the faith and laws of the universe that know no failure, your faith in the best of yourself (the principle of life in you) has brought you into conscious realization that you are not a victim of the universe, but a part of it. Consequently, there is that within yourself which is able to make conscious contact with the universal principal of law and power and enables you to press all the particular laws of nature, whether visible or invisible, into serving your particular demand or desire, and thereby you find yourself Master, not a slave of any situation.

Troward tells us that this Mastering is to be "accomplished by knowledge, and the only knowledge which will afford this purpose in all its measureless immensity is the knowledge of the personal element in universal spirit" and its reciprocity to our own personality. In other words, the words you think, the personality you feel yourself to be, are all reproductions in miniature or specialized God "or universal spirit." All your word-thoughts were God word-forms before they were yours.

The words you use are the instruments, channels, through which the creative energy takes shape. Naturally, this sensitive creative power can only reproduce in accordance with the instrument through which it passes. All disappointments and failures are the result of endeavoring to think one thing and produce another. This is just as impossible as it would be for an electric fan to be used for lighting purposes, or for water to flow through a crooked pipe in a straight line.

The water must take the shape of the pipe through which it flows. Even more truly this sensitive, invisible, fluent substance must reproduce outwardly the shape of the thought-word through which it passes. This is the law of its nature; therefore, it logically follows, "As a man thinketh, so is he." Hence, when your thought or word-form is in correspondence with the Eternal constructive and forward movement of the Universal Law, then your mind is the mirror in which the infinite power and intelligence of the universe sees itself reproduced, and your individual life becomes one of harmony.

CHAPTER 14

The Reward Of Increased Faith

It should be steadily borne in mind that there is an intelligence and power in all nature and all space that is always creative and infinitely sensitive and responsive. The responsiveness of its nature is two-fold: it is creative and amenable to suggestion. Once the human understanding grasps this all-important fact, it realizes the simplicity of the law of life.

All that is necessary is to realize that your mind is a center of Divine operation, and consequently contains that within itself which accepts suggestions, and expect all life to respond to your call, and you will find suggestions which tend to the fulfillment of your desire coming to you, not only from your fellowmen, but also from the flowers, the grass, the trees and the rocks which will enable you to fulfill your heart's desire, if you act upon them in confidence on this physical plane. "Faith without works is dead," but Faith with Works sets you absolutely free.

CHAPTER 15

Faith With Works - What It Has Accomplished

It is said of Tyson, the great Australian millionaire, that the suggestion to "make the desert land of Australia blossom as the rose" came to him from a modest little Australian violet while he was working as a bushman for something like three shillings a day. He used to find these friendly little violets growing in certain places in the woods, and something in the flower touched something akin to itself in the mind of Tyson, and he would sit on the side of his bunk at night and wonder how flowers and vegetable life could be given an opportunity to express itself in the desert land of Australia.

No doubt he realized that it would take a long time to save enough money to put irrigating ditches in the desert lands, but his thought and feeling were sure it could be accomplished, and if it could be done, he could do it. If there was a power within himself that was able to capture the idea, then there must be a responsive power within the idea itself that could bring itself into a practical physical manifestation. He resolutely put aside all questions as to the specific ways and means which would be employed in bringing his desire into physical manifestation, and simply kept his thought centered upon the idea of making fences and seeing flowers and grass where none existed.

Since the responsiveness of reproductive creative power is not limited to any local condition of mind, his habitual meditation and mental picture set his ideas free to roam in an infinitude and attract to themselves other ideas of a kindred nature. Therefore, it was not necessary for Tyson to wait and see his ideas and desires fulfilled, until he had saved from his three shillings a day enough money to irrigate the land, for his ideas found other ideas in the financial world which were attuned in sympathy with themselves, and doors of finance were quickly opened.

All charitable institutions are maintained upon the principle of the responsiveness of life. If this were not true, no one would care to give, simply because another needed. The law of demand and supply, cause and effect, can never be broken. Ideas attract to themselves kindred ideas. Sometimes they come from a flower, a book or out of the invisible. You are sitting or walking, intent upon an idea not quite complete as to the ways and means of fulfillment, and behold along comes another idea, from no one can tell where, and finds friendly lodging with your idea, one idea attracting another, and so on until your desires are physical facts.

You may feel the necessity for an improvement in your finances and wonder how this increase is to be brought about, when there seems suddenly to come from within the idea that everything had its birth in thought, even money, and your thoughts turn their course. You simply hold to the statement or affirmation that the best, and all there is, is yours. Since you are able to capture ideas from the Infinite through the instrument of your intuition, you let your mind rest upon that thought knowing full well that this very thought will respond to itself. Your inhibition of the thought of doubt and feeling of anxiety enables the reassuring ideas to establish themselves and attract to themselves "I can" and "I will" ideas, which gradually grow into physical form of the desire in mind.

In the conscious use of the universal power to reproduce your desires in physical form, three facts should be borne in mind:

First: All space is filled with a creative power.

Second: This creative power is amenable to suggestion.

Third: It can only work by deductive methods.

As Troward tells us, this last is an exceedingly important point, for it implies that the action of the ever-present creative power is in no way limited by precedent. It works according to the essence of the spirit of the principle. In other words, this universal power takes its creative direction from the word you give it. Once man realizes this great truth, it becomes the most important of all his consideration with what character this sensitive reproductive power is invested. It is the unvarying law of this creative life principle that "As a man thinketh in his heart so is he." If you realize the truth that the only creative power can be to you only what you feel and think it to be, it is willing and able to meet your demands.

Troward says, "If you think your thought is Powerful, then your Thought is Powerful." "As a man thinketh in his heart, so is he" is the law of life, and the creative power can no more change this law than an ordinary mirror can reflect back to you a different image than the object you hold before it. "As you think so are you" does not mean "as you tell people you think" or "as you would wish the world to believe you think." It means your innermost thoughts, that place where no one but you know. "None can know the father save the son" and "No one can know the son but the father."

Only the reproductive creative spirit of life knows what you think until your thoughts become physical facts and manifest themselves in your body, your brain or your affairs. Then everyone with whom you come into contact may know, because the father, the intelligent creative energy which heareth in secret, hears your most secret thoughts, rewards you openly, reproduces your thoughts in physical form. "As you think you know that is what you become" should be kept in the background of your mind constantly. This is watching and praying without ceasing, and when you are not feeling quite up to par to physically pray.

CHAPTER 16

Suggestions As To How To Pray Or Ask, Believing You Have Already Received

Scientific Thinking - Positive Thought

Suggestions for Practical Application:

Try, through careful, positive, enthusiastic (though not strenuous) thought, to realize that the indescribable, invisible substance of life fills all space; that its nature is intelligent, plastic, subjective substance.

Five o'clock in the morning is the best time to go into this sort of meditation. If you will retire early every night for one month, before falling asleep impress firmly upon your subjective mind the affirmation "My Father is the ruler of all the world, and is expressing His directing power through me," you will find that the substance of life takes form in the moulds of your thoughts.

Do not accept the above suggestion simply because it is given to you. Think it over carefully until the impression is made upon your own subconscious mind understandingly. Rise every morning, as was suggested before, at five o'clock, sit in a quiet room in a straight-backed chair, and think out the affirmation of the previous evening, and you will realize and be able to put into practice your princely power with the realization to some extent, at least, that your mind really is a center through which all the creative energy and power there is taking form.

Scientific Prayer:

The Principle Underlying Scientific Prayer

In prayer for a change in condition, physical, mental or financial for yourself or another, bear in mind that the fundamental necessity for the answer to prayer is the understanding of the scientific statement:

"Ask, BELIEVING YOU HAVE ALREADY RECEIVED, and you shall receive"

This is not as difficult as it appears on the surface, once you realize that everything has its origin in the mind, and that which you seek outwardly, you already possess. No one can think a thought in the future. Your thought of a thing constitutes its origin.

THEREFORE

The Thought Form of the Thing is already Yours as soon as you think it. Your steady recognition of this Thought Possession causes the thought to concentrate, to condense, to project itself and to assume physical form.

To Get Rich Through Creation

The recognition or conception of new forces of wealth is the loftiest aspiration you can take into your heart, for it assumes and implies the furtherance of all noble aims.

Items to be remembered about Prayer for Yourself or Another:

Remember that that which you call treatment or prayer is not, in any sense, hypnotism. It should never be your endeavor to take possession of the mind of another. Remember that it should never be your intention to make yourself believe that which you know to be untrue. You are simply thinking into God or First Cause with the understanding that -

"If a thing is true at all, there is a way in which it is true throughout the Universe." Remember that the Power of Thought works by absolutely scientific principles. These principles are expressed in the language of the statement:

"As a man thinketh in his heart, so is he."

This statement contains a world of wisdom, but man's steady recognition and careful application of the statement itself is required to bring it into practical use.

Remember that the principles, involved in being as we think in our heart are elucidated and revealed by the law "As you sow, you shall reap."

Remember that your Freedom to choose just what you will think, just what thought possession you will affirm, and claim constitutes God's gift to you.

It shows; How:

First Cause has endowed every man with the Power and Ability to bring into his personal environment whatever he chooses. Cause and Effect in reference to Getting:

If you plant an ACORN, you get an OAK. If you sow a GRAIN OF CORN, you reap a stalk and MANY Kernels of Corn. You always get the manifestation of that which you consciously or unconsciously AFFIRM and CLAIM, habitually declare and expect, or in other words "AS YOU SOW"

Therefore, sow the seeds of I AM...I OUGHT....I CAN...I WILL REALIZE that because you ARE you OUGHT, that because you OUGHT, you CAN, that because you CAN, you DO.

The manifestation of this Truth, even in a small degree, gives you the indisputable understanding that DOMINION IS YOUR CHARTER RIGHT You are an Heir of First Cause, endowed with all the power He has. God has given you everything. All is yours, and you know that all you have to do is to reach out your mental hand and take it.

This Formula may serve as a pattern to shape your own Prayer or Affirmation into God for the benefit of another or yourself.

If for another, you speak the Christian name of the person you wish to help, then dismiss their personality entirely from your consciousness.

Intensify your thought by meditating upon the fact that there is that in you which finds the way, which is the Truth and is the Life.

You are affirming this fact, believing that since you are thinking this, it is already yours. Having lifted up your feeling to the central idea of this meditation, you examine your own consciousness to see if there is ought which is unlike God. If there is any feeling of fear, worry, malice, envy, hatred, or jealousy, turn back in your meditation to Cleanse your Thought through the affirmation that God's Love and Purity fill all space including your heart and soul. Reconcile your thought with the Love of God, always remembering that

You are made in the Image and Likeness of Love.

Keep this Cleansing thought in mind until you feel that you have freed your consciousness entirely of all thoughts and feelings other than Love and Unity with all Humanity

Then if denials do not disturb you, deny all that is unlike your desired manifestation. This accomplished, you almost overlay your denial with the affirmative thought that: You are made in the Image and Likeness of God and that you already have your desire fulfilled in its first, its original spiritual or thought form.

Closing of Prayer:

Prayer as a method of thought is a deliberate use of the Law which gives you the Power of Dominion over everything which tends in any way to hamper your perfect liberty. YOU HAVE BEEN GIVEN LIFE THAT YOU MAY ENJOY IT MORE AND MORE FULLY The steady recognition of this Truth makes you declare yourself a PRINCE OF POWER.

You recognize, accept and use this power as A CHILD OF A KING AND HENCE DOMINION IS YOUR BIRTHRIGHT Then when you feel the light of this great Truth flooding your consciousness open the floodgates of your soul in Heartfelt Praise that you have the understanding that THE CREATOR AND HIS CREATION ARE ONE.

Also, that the Creator is continually creating through his creation.

Close your treatment in the happy assurance that the Prayer which is fulfilled is not a form of supplication but a steady habitual affirming that The Creator of all Creation is operating Specifically through you, therefore

THE WORK MUST BE PERFECTLY DONE, YOUR MIND IS A CENTER OF DIVINE OPERATION.

Hints for Application and Practice:

For every five minutes given to reading and study of the theories of Mental Science, spend fifteen minutes in the use and application of the knowledge acquired.

1. Spend one minute in every twenty-four hours in

conscientiously thinking over the specification that must be observed in order to have your prayers answered.

2. Practice the steady recognition of desirable thought possession for two periods of fifteen minutes each every day. Not only time yourself each period to see how long you can keep a given conception before your mental vision, but also keep a written record of the vividness with which you experience your mental image. Remember that your mental senses are just as varied and trainable as your physical ones.

3. Spend five minutes every day between 12 noon and 1 o'clock with a mental search for new sources of wealth.

CHAPTER 17

Things to Remember

Remember that the greatest Mental Scientist the world has ever known (Jesus Christ, the Man) said all things are possible unto you.

Also, the "things I do you can do." Did he tell the truth?

Jesus did not claim to be more divine than you are. He declared the whole human race children of God. By birth he was no 'exception to this rule. The power he possessed was developed through His personal effort. He said you could do the same if you would only believe in yourself. A great idea is valueless unless accompanied by physical action. God gives the idea; man works it out upon the physical plane.

All that is really worthwhile is contentment. Self-command alone can produce it. The soul and body are one. Contentment of mind is contentment of soul, and contentment of soul means contentment of body.

If you wish health, watch your thoughts, not only of your physical being, but your thoughts about everything and everybody. With your will keep them in line with your desire, and outwardly act in accordance with your thoughts, and you will soon realize that all power both over thoughts and conditions has been given to you. You believe in God. Believe in yourself as the physical instrument through which God operates. Absolute dominion is yours when you have sufficient self-mastery to conquer the negative tendency of thoughts and actions.

Ask yourself daily: "What is the purpose of the power which put me here?" "How can I work with the purpose for life and liberty in me?"

Upon having decided these questions, endeavor hourly to fulfill them.

You are a law unto yourself.

If you have a tendency to overdo anything, eat, drink or blame circumstances for your misfortunes, conquer that tendency with the inward conviction that all power is yours outwardly. Eat less, drink less, blame circumstances less, and the best there is will gradually grow in the place where the worst seemed to be.

Always remember that all is yours to use, as you will. You can if you will: if you will you do.

God the Father blesses you with all He has to give.

Make good Godly use of it.

The reason for greater success when you first began your studies and demonstrations in Mental Science is that your joy and enthusiasm at the simple discovery of the power within was greater than you have been able to put into your understanding later.

With increased understanding put increasing joy and enthusiasm, and the results will correspond.

LIST OF TITLES WITH ISBN NO.

ISBN	TITLE
9788194914129	1984
9789390575220	1984 & Animal Farm (2In1)
9789390575572	1984 & Animal Farm (2In1): The International Best-Selling Classics
9789390575848	35 Sonnets
9789390575329	A Clergyman's Daughter
9789390575923	A Study In Scarlet
9789390896097	A Tale Of Two Cities
9789390896837	Abide in Christ
9789390896202	Abraham Lincoln
9789390896912	Absolute Surrender
9789390896608	African American Classic Collection
9789390575305	Aldous Huxley: The Collected Works
9789390896141	An Autobiography of M. K. Gandhi
9789390575886	Animal Farm
9789390575619	Animal Farm & The Great Gatsby (2In1)
9789390575626	Animal Farm & We
9789390896158	Anna Karenina
9789390575534	Antic Hay
9789390896165	Antony & Cleopatra
9789390896172	As I Lay Dying
9789390896226	As You like it
9789390575671	At Your Command
9789390575350	Awakened Imagination
9789390575114	Be What You Wish
9789390896233	Believe In yourself
9789390896998	Best of Charles Darwin: The Origin of Species & Autobiography
9789390896684	Best Of Horror : Dracula And Frankenstein
9789390575503	Best Of Mark Twain (The Adventures of Tom Sawyer AND The Adventures of Huckleberry Finn)
9789390896769	Black History Collection
9789390575756	Brave New World, Animal Farm & 1984 (3in1)

9789390896240	Brother Karamzov
9789390575053	Bulleh Shah Poetry
9789390575725	Burmese Days
9789390896257	Bushido
9789390896066	Can't Hurt Me
9788194914112	Chanakya Neeti: With The Complete Sutras
9789390896042	Crime and Punishment
9789390575527	Crome Yellow
9789390575046	Down and Out in Paris and London
9789390896844	Dracula
9789390575442	Emersons Essays: The Complete First & Second Series (Self-Reliance & Other Essays)
9789390575749	Emma
9789390575817	Essential Tozer Collection - The Pursuit of God & The Purpose of Man
9789390896578	Fascism What It Is and How to Fight It
9789390575688	Feeling is the Secret
9789390575190	Five Lessons
9789390575954	Frankenstein
9789390575237	Franz Kafka: Collected Works
9789390575282	Franz Kafka: Short Stories
9789390575060	George Orwell Collected Works
9789390575077	George Orwell Essays
9789390575213	George Orwell Poems
9788194914150	Greatest Poetry Ever Written Vol 1
9788194914143	Greatest Poetry Ever Written Vol 1
9789390896301	Gulliver's Travel
9789390575961	Gunaho Ka Devta
9789390575893	H. P. Lovecraft Selected Stories Vol 1
9789390575978	H. P. Lovecraft Selected Stories Vol 2
9789390896059	Hamlet
9789390575022	His Last Bow: Some Reminiscences of Sherlock Holmes
9789390896134	History of Western Philosophy
9789390575121	Homage To Catalonia

9789390896219	How to develop self-confidence and Improve public Speaking
9789390896295	How to enjoy your life and your Job
9789390575633	How to own your own mind
9789390896318	How to read Human Nature
9789390896325	How to sell your way through the life
9789390896370	How to use the laws of mind
9789390896387	How to use the power of prayer
9789390896028	How to win friends & Influence People
9788194824176	How To Win Friends and Influence People
9789390896103	Humility The Beauty of Holiness
9789390896653	Imperialism the Highest Stage of Capitalism
9789390575084	In Our Time
9789390575169	In Our Time & Three Stories and Ten poems
9789390575145	James Allen: The Collected Works
9789390896189	Jesus Himself
9789390575480	Jo's Boys
9789390896394	Julius Caesar
9789390575404	Keep the Aspidistra Flying
9789390896400	Kidnapped
9789390896424	King Lear
9789390575824	Lady Susan
9789390896455	Law of Success
9789390896264	Lincoln The Unknown
9789390575565	Little Men
9789390575640	Little Women
9788194914174	Lost Horizon
9789390896462	Macbeth
9789390896929	Man Eaters of Kumaon
9789390896523	Man The Dwelling Place of God
9789390896349	Man The Dwelling Place of God
9789390575909	Mansfield Park
9788194914136	Manto Ki 25 Sarvshreshth Kahaniya
9789390896509	Marxism, Anarchism, Communism
9789390575664	Mathematical Principles of Natural Philosophy

9788194914198	Meditations
9789390575800	Mein Kampf
9789390575794	Memory How To Develop, Train, And Use It
9789390896486	Mind Power
9789390896585	Money
9789390575039	Mortal Coils
9789390575770	My Life and Work
9789390896035	Narrative of the Life of Frederick Douglass
9789390575152	Neville Goddard: The Collected Works
9789390575985	Northanger Abbey
9789390896530	Notes From Underground
9789390896547	Oliver Twist
9789390575459	On War
9789390575541	One, None and a Hundred Thousand
9789390896554	Othelo
9789390575435	Out Of This World
9789390575015	Persuasion
9789390575510	Prayer The Art Of Believing
9789390575091	Pride and Prejudice
9789390896561	Psychic Perception
9789390575381	Rabindranath Tagore - 5 Best Short Stories Vol 2
9789390575367	Rabindranath Tagore - Short Stories (Masters Collections Including The Childs Return)
9789390575374	Rabindranath Tagore 5 Best Short Stories Vol 1 (Including The Childs Return
9789390896622	Romeo & Juliet
9789390896127	Sanatana Dharma
9789390575596	Seedtime & Harvest
9789390896639	Selected Stories of Guy De Maupassant
9789390575206	Self-Reliance & Other Essays
9789390575176	Sense and Sensibility
9789390575299	Shyamchi Aai
9789390896738	Socialism Utopian and Scientific
9789390896646	Success Through a Positive Mental Attitude
9789390575428	The Adventures of Huckleberry Finn

9789390575183	The Adventures of Sherlock Holmes
9789390575343	The Adventures of Tom Sawyer
9789390896691	The Alchemy Of Happiness
9789390575862	The Art Of Public Speaking
9789390896288	The Autobiography Of Charles Darwin
9788194914181	The Best of Franz Kafka: The Metamorphosis & The Trial
9789390575008	The Call Of Cthulhu and Other Weird Tales
9789390575107	The Case-Book of Sherlock Holmes
9789390896110	The Castle Of Otranto
9789390896745	The Communist Manifesto
9789390575589	The Complete Fiction of H. P. Lovecraft
9789390575497	The Complete Works of Florence Scovel Shinn
9789390896820	The Conquest of Breard
9789390896813	The Diary of a Young Girl
9789390896332	The Diary of a Young Girl The Definitive Edition of the Worlds Most Famous Diary
9789390575701	The Great Gatsby, Animal Farm & 1984 (3In1)
9789390575312	The Greatest Works Of George Orwell (5 Books) Including 1984 & Non-Fiction
9789390575992	The Hound of Baskervilles
9789390896707	The Idiot
9789390896714	The Invisible Man
9789390575657	The Knowledge of the holy
9789390575558	The Law & the Promise
9789390896721	The Law Of Attraction
9789390896776	The Leader in you
9789390896363	The Life of Christ
9789390896196	The Man-Eating Leopard of Rudraprayag
9789390896783	The Master Key to Riches
9789390575268	The Memoirs Of Sherlock Holmes
9789390896479	The Midsummer Night's Dream
9789390575466	The Mill On The Floss
9789390896790	The Miracles of your mind
9789390896660	The Mutual Aid A Factor in Evolution
9789390896448	The Origin of Species

9789390896905	The Peter Kropotkin Anthology The Conquest of Bread & Mutual Aid A Factor of Evolution
9789390896806	The Picture of Dorian Gray
9789390896271	The Picture of Dorian Gray
9789390575275	The Power Of Awareness
9789390896356	The Power of Concentration
9788194824169	The Power of Positive Thinking
9789390575411	The Power of the Spoken Word
9788194914105	The Power Of Your Subconscious Mind
9789390896899	The Power of Your Subconscious Mind
9789390896417	The Principles of Communism
9789390575787	The Psychology Of Mans Possible Evolution
9789390896615	The Psychology of Salesmanship
9789390575732	The Pursuit of God
9789390575398	The Pursuit of Happiness
9789390896851	The Quick and Easy Way to effective Speaking
9789390575947	The Return Of Sherlock Holmes
9789390575138	The Road To Wigan Pier
9789390896981	The Root of the Righteous
9789390575855	The Science Of Being Well
9788194914167	The Science Of Getting Rich, The Science Of Being Great & The Science Of Being Well (3In1)
9789390896011	The Screwtape Letters
9789390896073	The Screwtape Letters
9789390575336	The Secret Door to Success
9789390575695	The Secret Of Imagining
9789390896868	The Secret Of Success
9789390896431	The Seven Last Words
9789390575930	The Sign of the Four
9789390896004	The Sonnets
9789390896516	The Souls of Black Folk
9789390896875	The Sound and The Fury
9789390575244	The State and Revolution
9789390896882	The Story of My Life
9789390896936	The Story Of Oriental Philosophy

9789390896752	The Strange Case of Dr. Jekyll and Mr. Hyde
9789390896943	The Tempest
9789390575916	The Valley Of Fear
9789390575879	The Wind in the willows
9789390896080	The Wind in the willows
9789390575763	Their eyes were watching gofd
9789390575831	Three Stories
9789390896950	Twelfth Night
9789390896592	Twelve Years a Slave
9789390896677	Up from Slavery
9789390896974	Value Price and Profit
9789390896967	Wake Up and Live
9789390896493	With Christ in the School of Prayer
9789390575602	Your Faith is Your Fortune
9789390575473	Your Infinite Power To Be Rich
9789390575251	Your Word is Your Wand
9789390575718	Youth
9789391316099	A Christmas Carol
9789391316105	A Doll's House
9789391316501	A Passage to India
9789391316709	A Portrait of the Artist as a Young Man
9789391316112	A Tale of Two Cities
9789391316747	A Tear and a Smile
9789391316167	Agnes Gray
9789391316174	Alice's Adventures in Wonderland
9789391316136	Anandamath
9789391316181	Anne Of Green Gables
9789391316754	Anthem
9789391316198	Around The World in 80 Days
9789391316013	As A Man Thinketh
9789391316242	Autobiography of a Yogi
9789391316266	Beyond Good and Evil
9789391316761	Bleak House
9789391316778	Chitra, a Play in One Act
9789391316310	David Copperfield

9789391316075	Demian
9789391316785	Dubliners
9789391316051	Favourite Tales from the Arabian Nights
9789391316235	Gitanjali
9789391316068	Gravity
9789391316150	Great Speeches of Abraham Lincoln
9789391316662	Guerilla Warfare
9789391316839	Kim
9789391316822	Mother
9789391316211	My Childhood
9789391316846	Nationalism
9789391316327	Oliver Twist
9789391316853	Pygmalion
9789391316334	Relativity: The Special and the General Theory
9789391316389	Scientific Healing Affirmation
9789391316341	Sons and Lovers
9789391316587	Tales from India
9789391316372	Tess of The D'Urbervilles
9789391316396	The Awakening and Selected Stories
9789391316402	The Bhagvad Gita
9789391316303	The Book of Enoch
9789391316228	The Canterville Ghost
9789391316907	The Dynamic Laws of Prosperity
9789391316006	The Great Gatsby
9789391316860	The Hungry Stones and Other Stories
9789391316433	The Idiot
9789391316440	The Importance of Being Earnest
9789391316297	The Light of Asia
9789391316914	The Madman His Parables and Poems
9789391316457	The Odyssey
9789391316921	The Picture of Dorian Gray
9789391316464	The Prince
9789391316938	The Prophet
9789391316945	The Republic
9789391316518	The Scarlet Letter

9789391316143	The Seven Laws of Teaching
9789391316525	The Story of My Experiments with Truth
9789391316532	The Tales of the Mother Goose
9789391316549	The Thirty Nine Steps
9789391316594	The Time Machine
9789391316600	The Turn of the Screw
9789391316983	The Upanishads
9789391316617	The Yellow Wallpaper
9789391316426	The Yoga Sutras of Patanjali
9789391316990	Ulysses
9789391316624	Utopia
9789391316679	Vanity Fair
9789391316020	What Is To Be Done
9789391316686	Within A Budding Grove
9789391316693	Women in Love